LANGUAGE ARTS EXPLORER

LOCAL FARMS AND SUSTAINABLE FOODS

by Julia Vogel

CHERRY LAKE PUBLISHING • ANN ARBOR, MICHIGAN

Published in the United States of America
by Cherry Lake Publishing
Ann Arbor, Michigan
www.cherrylakepublishing.com

Printed in the United States of America
Corporate Graphics Inc
January 2010
CLSP06

Consultants: Karen O'Connor, co-owner, Mother Earth Gardens, Minneapolis, Minnesota; Gail Saunders-Smith, associate professor of literacy, Beeghly College of Education, Youngstown State University

Editorial direction: Book design and illustration:
Melissa Johnson   Becky Daum

Photo credits: Dallas Events Inc/Shutterstock Images, cover, 1; Fotolia, 5, 20, 24; Petr Nad/Fotolia, 7; Suprijono Suharjoto/Fotolia, 9; Oleg Kozlov/Fotolia, 11; Vonora/Fotolia, 12; Liza McCorkle/iStockphoto, 15; Ralf Wachter/Fotolia, 16; Penny Williams/Fotolia, 19; Igor Kisseley/Fotolia, 23; RichG/Fotolia, 27

Library of Congress Cataloging-in-Publication Data
Vogel, Julia.
  Save the planet : Local farms and sustainable foods / by Julia Vogel.
     p. cm. — (Language arts explorer)
  Includes index.
  ISBN 978-1-60279-660-7 (hardback) — ISBN 978-1-60279-669-0 (pbk.)
  1. Sustainable agriculture—Juvenile literature. 2. Farms, Small—Juvenile literature. I. Title. II. Series.

  S494.5.S86V64 2010
  630—dc22

2009038096

Cherry Lake Publishing would like to acknowledge the work of The Partnership for 21st Century Skills. Please visit www.21centuryskills.org for more information.

TABLE OF CONTENTS

You are being given a mission. The facts in What You Know will help you accomplish it. Remember What You Know while you are reading the story. The story will help you answer the questions at the end of the book. Have fun on this adventure!

Your mission is to investigate how food is grown on farms. Everyone needs to eat. Supermarkets offer many food choices every day. But many people worry about the ways fruits, vegetables, and other foods are grown. Some farming methods can be unhealthy for us and harmful to the planet. Are there ways for farmers to grow food that are better for our health and the planet? Join our investigation of a small fruit and vegetable farm in Maryland. Just remember What You Know as you learn about farms.

WHAT YOU KNOW

★ In earlier times, many people ate food that they grew themselves or bought from small local farms. Now, more of the food we eat comes from huge farms that produce one type of crop.

★ Runoff happens when there is too much water to soak into the ground. Runoff from farms can include chemicals that wash off fields during storms. Runoff is the biggest cause of water pollution in many places.

Some farmers spray their crops with chemicals.

★ Chemicals that farmers use can be found on fruits and vegetables at the supermarket. Some chemicals may be dangerous if people eat or breathe too much of them over a long period of time.

★ Food may travel thousands of miles between the farm where it grew and your plate. This can be a problem because transportation uses a lot of energy, which causes pollution.

We'll be following a student who is working on a small, organic farm. Come along!

Maryland weather in February is awful! It's gray, icy, and freezing cold. The leafless trees make it seem like no plants could grow here. But at the supermarket this morning, the produce aisle was piled high with fruits and vegetables. The red apples and green grapes looked like a tasty winter snack.

Traveling Food

But then I looked closer. A sticker on the apples said, "Product of New Zealand." The grapes were labeled, "Grown in Chile." That means my snack could have traveled 8,000 miles (12,800 km) to get to my mouth. Shipping food around the world allows people to eat foods that don't grow nearby. When it is winter in the United States, people there can eat food grown in South America or other places where it is summer. However, it takes a lot of energy for food to travel so far.

Next, I noticed something about the fruits' skin. No bruises, bumps, or brown spots. The fruit seemed too perfect. Many farms use human-made chemicals to grow produce without diseases or insect damage. It takes a lot of these chemicals, plus fuel energy, to keep the produce looking perfect while it's shipped.

Some fruits and vegetables travel a long way to get to the supermarket.

Grown Locally

Many families used to grow food on their own land without artificial chemicals. Many people still believe that growing food locally, without artificial chemicals, is healthier for humans and the earth. This farming method is called sustainable because it keeps, or sustains, the land's ability to grow food without damaging the environment. I want to find out how sustainable farming works.

Meeting a Farmer

After doing some research online, I got in touch with a nearby organic farmer. I volunteered to help out on her farm so I could learn more about sustainable farming.

LOCAL FARMS, LOCAL CLIMATES

The local climate affects when and how food is grown, whether you're planting in your backyard or on thousands of acres. Maryland is on the East Coast of the United States. It has a five-month growing season. Farmers have learned which crops grow well in Maryland and when to plant them. Farmers in other places, with more or less sun or rain, grow different crops or the same crops in different ways.

First, I learned some definitions. Local food means that the food was grown nearby. Organic means that the food was grown without using certain chemicals. Local food is not always organic, depending on the choices the farmer makes. The organic food you find in the supermarket is not always local. Big companies in the United States and as far away as China ship organic food to grocery stores everywhere. Sustainable food is both local and organic. Growing and shipping sustainable food does as little damage to the planet as possible. ★

Organic produce in the supermarket might not be locally grown.

Today was amazing! I spent the afternoon in rubber boots digging in the dirt at Fox Hill Farm. Actually, the farm owner, Daisy Stevens, says I was digging in soil, not dirt. Soil is a mixture of living and nonliving matter that plants depend on to grow. And she should know. Her family has been farming this soil for one hundred years.

Crops Need Nutrients

I didn't think they'd put me to work so soon, but farm chores start before the planting season. The first step is to test the soil. Growing crops takes nutrients out of the ground. Good farmers test the soil every year to learn what's missing from it. A conventional farmer will buy artificial chemicals to replace the needed nutrients. It is cheaper, easier, and grows more food at first than organic methods.

But those chemical fertilizers wash off in spring rains. The chemical fertilizers are made from fossil fuels including oil. Oil is a nonrenewable resource. That means someday we will use it up. Fossil fuels also cause pollution. Fertilizer runoff pollutes the water in lakes and rivers and causes too much algae to grow in them. This makes it harder

Farming is hard work!

When too many fertilizer chemicals get into the water, too much algae grows.

for underwater plants and animals to live. Where I live, fertilizer pollution creates dead zones in the Chesapeake Bay, where crabs, oysters, and other sea life are dying out.

Keeping the Land Fertile

Fox Hill is an organic farm. The farmers use nonchemical methods to keep their land fertile. Fertile soil has a balance of nutrients and minerals. It includes enough water and small organisms to keep plants healthy. Farmers rotate their crops, which means they grow different crops in each field every year. Different crops use different nutrients in the soil. Rotating crops each year helps make sure that the nutrients do not get used up completely. When organic farmers need to make the soil more fertile, they add compost. Compost is a decaying mix of leaves, manure, and other natural things that rot.

Today, we spread compost on vegetable plots. It is rich with nutrients plants need. My very first shovelful turned up five earthworms. Worms are wiggly signs of healthy soil that's getting healthier. ★

ORGANIC, OR OFFICIALLY ORGANIC?

Organic produce farming is usually defined as growing food plants without chemical fertilizers, pesticides, or other artificial chemicals. The U.S. government certifies organic farms. Many small farmers use organic methods but do not have official certification. At the farmers' market, ask the farmers if they are certified organic or use organic methods. Remember, not all local or small farms are organic, and not all organic food is local.

During a trip last summer, I saw conventional farms with endless acres of corn. Fox Hill's owner, Daisy, tells me that's called a monoculture. Conventional farmers often grow one crop because their fields are tended by heavy machines. It's easy to drive a tractor down one long row after another. One worker can do the whole job.

Fox Hill and other small organic farms use fewer machines. At these farms, more people do farm work. Instead of spending money on tractors and gas, the farm pays local workers. That keeps money in the neighborhood, which makes these farms good for the local economy.

Today we're planting tomato seedlings with odd names like Cherokee Purple, Black Plum, and Green Zebra. You

FARMING IN THE CITY

Country farms are not the only places where people grow local or organic food. Many urban and suburban areas have community gardens. Communities build gardens in parks, in abandoned lots, or even on rooftops. Volunteers work together and share the produce when it is ready to harvest. Some community gardens even sell their produce at local markets. Many people grow organic food in their own backyards, too.

Heirloom tomatoes come in different sizes, shapes, and colors.

can't usually buy these kinds of tomatoes in supermarkets. Conventional tomatoes have to be sturdy because they are harvested by machines and trucked to market. The tomatoes we grow come in many colors, shapes, and flavors, from sweet to spicy to lemon-lime.

Heirloom Food

Through history, farmers have bred different varieties of plants to grow in different places and to satisfy different tastes. But now many varieties are dying out because conventional farms don't grow them. Luckily, a few farms save the seeds from the old breeds, just like family antiques. These are called heirloom breeds. These breeds are well adapted to their local areas—and they taste fantastic! ★

Farmers have to work really hard to grow their crops! They spend a lot of time dealing with weeds. A weed is any plant that grows where you don't want it to. On farms, weeds compete with crops for water and nutrients in the soil. Some, like thistles, grow fast and tall enough to shade other plants.

Herbicides

A farmer with a huge farm probably couldn't pull acres of weeds by hand. Instead, conventional farmers

Thistles can interfere with a farmer's crops.

often attack weeds with chemicals. Chemicals that kill all kinds of farm pests are called pesticides, and the kinds of pesticides that kill weeds are called herbicides. Some herbicides stay on the food plants, wash into streams, or collect in the soil. It can be dangerous if a person breathes or eats a lot of herbicides over time. Herbicides can cause serious problems ranging from skin rashes to cancer.

Other Ways to Fight Weeds

At Fox Hill, I've learned to use lots of different weed-control methods. Spreading straw mulch keeps weeds away from the squashes. Vinegar kills weeds under the blueberries. A few weeds, such as dandelions, even get sold for people to eat. And we hoe and pull other weeds to make sure they don't spread. ★

Buzzing and chirping insects are everywhere in June, munching leaves and sucking plant juices. Bugs can drive farmers nuts. Conventional farmers use pesticides to protect their crops from insects. Pesticides that kill insects are called insecticides. Leftovers from these long-lasting chemicals are called residues. Residues can pollute soil and tap water.

Outsmarting Bugs

Daisy and other organic farmers outsmart pests without chemicals. Daisy explains that planting one huge field of a grasshopper's favorite food is like inviting 10,000

INSECT POISONS DON'T JUST POISON INSECTS

When wildlife eat insects poisoned by pesticides, they can be poisoned, too. A powerful insecticide called DDT protected crops starting in the 1940s. People soon found out that DDT also killed other animals. Some birds began to lay thin-shelled eggs. The young birds could not hatch and instead died. The United States made DDT illegal in 1972, which saved bald eagles and other birds from disappearing.

Some farmers use chemicals to keep insects out of crops.

over for dinner, so she grows lots of different kinds of plants. Crop rotation helps, too, because many pests stay in the soil through the winter. If potato-eating insects come out of the soil in spring and find only celery to eat, they starve. Sprinkling ground-up oyster shells on the soil keeps cutworms off cabbages. And tomato hornworms are so big and slow that people can pluck them off by hand.

Organic farmers even put other animals to work at insect control. Whereas insecticides kill good bugs as well as bad, organic farming methods let helpful insects survive. Insect-eating birds and bats are encouraged to help, too. Chickens peck and scratch for beetle larvae in vegetable patches. The bird droppings then fertilize the garden. ★

Daisy tells me that a healthy farm doesn't fight against nature. Organic farmers look at their land as being a part of nature. That means leaving some of the land wild.

Natural Benefits

Patches of wildflowers grow tall beside fields not sprayed with herbicides. Plants such as milkweed and goldenrod attract bees and butterflies. Bees and butterflies help apples and other farm crops grow. Many wild plants also grow deep roots. Deep roots are helpful because they

A healthy farm is part of nature.

WHAT'S HAPPENING TO HONEYBEES?

Since 2006, colonies of honeybees have been dying mysteriously around the world. Many plants need bees to move pollen from one plant to another to produce fruit. Scientists are trying to figure out what is killing the bees. Disease, stress, and pesticides are some of the suspects. Scientists need to learn more about the effects of pesticides on bees and other living creatures.

hold tightly to farm soil. Plowed ground loses soil, or erodes, in every rainstorm. Borders of wild plants slow erosion, keeping soil where it belongs instead of washing downstream.

Animals are attracted to Fox Hill's clean water and wild plants. Some animals are good for the farm. For example, some snakes eat mice and rats. Other wild animals can cause problems around farm crops, though. It costs money to put up rabbit-proof fences and bird nets to protect the berries. Allowing wildlife in is another way in which sustainable farming is connected to the natural patterns of life. Everyone around here says they wouldn't like Fox Hill as much if they never saw foxes. ★

Peaches. Blackberries. Corn. Watermelons and cantaloupes. Tomatoes, tomatoes, and more tomatoes. Once a week, we load the truck and head to the town farmers' market. It makes sense, says Daisy, to sell directly to consumers. Fox Hill gets to keep more of the money from sales than farms selling to supermarkets. The market is also a chance to meet other local farmers, to see what grew well for them this year, and get ideas on ways to improve next year.

Treats from the Market

It's especially fun to watch first-time customers. They move from stand to stand, loading up on honey, cider, flowers, eggs, and homemade breads and pies. At our table, some just stare at the tomatoes. Our heirloom tomatoes are brick red, pink, orange, green striped, or black. When I slice up a juicy sample, the customers can't resist!

It's easier for many customers to shop at a grocery store. Organic food in supermarkets and in farmers' markets is usually more expensive than conventional food, too. I asked a few customers why they come to the market and choose organic food. "I like to meet the farmer who

Some farmers sell their crops at local farmers' markets.

At farmers' markets, customers can meet the farmers who grew the food.

grew my food," said one woman. "It helps me trust that it's safe to eat."

"I'm a bird-watcher," said a man. "I want to support farming that's good for the environment."

"The apples don't always look perfect," admitted another customer. "But even with a few brown spots, they make great applesauce."

A mom pushing a stroller told me, "It's healthier to eat food that's fresh, that isn't sprayed with chemicals or stored for days before we eat it. And my kids eat more fruits and vegetables when the food tastes good."

Making a Difference

I'm going to keep volunteering on the farm throughout the harvest season. There's plenty more I want to learn about sustainable farming in Maryland and around the world. But I've already learned that the food we eat affects our health and our environment. If eating peaches ripe off a tree is good for me, for wildlife, and for my community, I'm happy to help. It's a delicious way to make a difference. ★

MISSION ACCOMPLISHED!

Great job! You have learned a lot about how food is grown on farms. Now you know that farmers can use many methods to protect human health, avoid polluting, and help wildlife. You know that eating food grown close to home saves shipping costs—and tastes terrific. Congratulations on a successful and delicious mission. Happy sustainable eating!

CONSIDER THIS

Consider the benefits of eating sustainable foods. By asking yourself more questions about sustainable farming, you might just start a mission of your own!

★ How does eating local fruits and vegetables save energy?

★ How does organic farming protect water quality, wildlife, and nature?

★ When you buy from a farmers' market, how are you helping the local community?

★ Why do people choose sustainable food?

Why do people choose local or organic food?

★ Have you eaten sustainable foods before? If so, what were they and how did they taste?

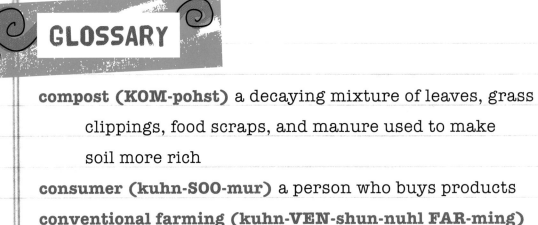

GLOSSARY

compost (KOM-pohst) a decaying mixture of leaves, grass clippings, food scraps, and manure used to make soil more rich

consumer (kuhn-SOO-mur) a person who buys products

conventional farming (kuhn-VEN-shun-nuhl FAR-ming) a method of farming that uses chemical fertilizers and pesticides

crop rotation (KROP roh-TAY-shun) a system of raising different crops on the same land in different seasons or different years

erosion (i-ROH-zhuhn) washing away or wearing away of soil by water or wind

fertilizer (FUR-tuh-lize-ur) a natural or artificial substance added to soil to help plants grow

heirloom (AIR-loom) an antique variety of plant or animal

herbicide (UR-buh-side) chemical used to kill plants considered to be pests

insecticide (in-SEKT-uh-side) chemical used to kill insects considered to be pests

monoculture (MON-uh-kuhl-chur) a farming practice that grows only one kind of plant in an area at a time

nutrient (NOO-tree-uhnt) a mineral or a chemical needed by a living thing to stay healthy

pesticide (PESS-tuh-side) chemical used to kill insects, plants, or animals considered to be pests

residue (REZ-uh-doo) tiny pieces or a coating of something that is left behind

LEARN MORE

BOOKS

Buller, Laura. *Food*. London: DK, 2005.

Reynolds, Jan. *Cycle of Rice, Cycle of Life: A Story of Sustainable Farming*. New York, NY: Lee & Low, 2009.

Sanger, Rick, and Carol Russell. *No Eat Not Food*. Grass Valley, CA: Mountain Path Press, 2006.

WEB SITES

Local Harvest
http://www.localharvest.org
Find a farmers' market near you.

Organic.org
http://www.organic.org
Learn more about organic food.

FURTHER MISSIONS

DRAW A MAP TO YOUR REFRIGERATOR

Look inside your refrigerator. Pick a few fresh fruits or vegetables. Can you tell where they were grown? Get your parents' permission to go online and research farming practices where the food was grown. Then draw a map that shows the path between where the food came from and your house. Do you think the food traveled by ship, train, plane, or truck? How long do you think the trip took? Are there similar foods you could eat instead that are grown closer to home?

DARE TO COMPARE

During your local apple harvest season, buy different kinds of apples at a local farm or market, plus some apples from a grocery store. Label the fruits with letters so other people do not know which one came from where. Then ask family members or friends to look at the fruits and decide which one looks the best. Next, ask everyone to taste the apples. Which one tastes the sweetest? The juiciest? The crunchiest? Finally, compare notes. Does everyone like the same kind of apple? If your favorite apple was grown nearby, the farmer who grew it would like to know.

INDEX

ABOUT THE AUTHOR

Julia Vogel, PhD, is a freelance writer and author of award-winning children's books. When she isn't hiking or bird-watching with her family, she grows organic tomatoes in her Maryland backyard.

ABOUT THE CONSULTANTS

Karen O'Connor is a gardening and local food advocate from Minnesota. She is co-owner of Mother Earth Gardens in Minneapolis, an independent garden center focusing on organic and sustainable gardening. She lives with her husband, two sons, and several small pets.

Gail Saunders-Smith is a former classroom teacher and Reading Recovery teacher leader. Currently she teaches literacy courses at Youngstown State University in Ohio. Gail is the author of many books for children and three professional books for teachers.